"This small book is b   [barcode]
gender identity, and S.
tantly, he helps readers go deep in understanding why the God
who created us wants us to flourish as the creatures we are, and
he equips readers to accompany those who struggle with this
life-giving truth."

> **Ryan T. Anderson,** President, Ethics and Public Policy
> Center; author, *When Harry Became Sally: Responding to
> the Transgender Moment*

"Loaded with practical advice, this book is a must-read for
those who struggle with gender identity—and for their parents,
youth leaders, and pastors. Ferguson's academic work, pastoral
experiences, and clear thinking uniquely position him to bring
clarity and compassion to a movement that is often muddled
and full of pain. If you're trying to understand the transgender
phenomenon and think about it biblically, this book's for you."

> **Sarah Eekhoff Zylstra,** Senior Writer, The Gospel
> Coalition; editor, *Social Sanity in an Insta World*

"In this book, Sam Ferguson engages basic questions facing many today. Is our identity as male and female fundamentally oppressive or creative? Should we change the body to heal the mind? What's the answer to current hurts and pains? How does transitioning compare with the Bible's promise of transformation? Whose voices are informing and shaping minds today on these issues? Ferguson addresses these questions and more with compassion, clarity, humility, respect, and helpful guidance."

Mark Dever, Pastor, Capitol Hill Baptist Church, Washington, DC

"Sam Ferguson's *Does God Care about Gender Identity?* exhibits a rare combination of pastoral wisdom, intellectual brilliance, and compassionate engagement of the culture. Highly recommended!"

Andreas Köstenberger, Founder, Biblical Foundations; Theologian in Residence, Fellowship Raleigh; author, *God, Marriage, and Family*

"In an era of gender and sexual confusion, Sam Ferguson has written a refreshing examination of the Bible's perspective, providing clear and articulate understanding for the Christ follower."

Foley Beach, Archbishop, Anglican Church in North America

Does God Care about Gender Identity?

TGC Hard Questions

Jared Kennedy, Series Editor

Does God Care about Gender Identity?

Samuel D. Ferguson

CROSSWAY®

WHEATON, ILLINOIS

Does God Care about Gender Identity?

Copyright © 2023 by Samuel D. Ferguson

Published by Crossway
        1300 Crescent Street
        Wheaton, Illinois 60187

Cover design: Ben Stafford

Cover images: Unsplash

First printing 2023

Printed in the United States of America

Scripture quotations are from the ESV® Bible (The Holy Bible, English Standard Version®), copyright © 2001 by Crossway, a publishing ministry of Good News Publishers. Used by permission. All rights reserved. The ESV text may not be quoted in any publication made available to the public by a Creative Commons license. The ESV may not be translated into any other language.

All emphases in Scripture quotations have been added by the author.

Trade paperback ISBN: 978-1-4335-9115-0
ePub ISBN: 978-1-4335-9117-4
PDF ISBN: 978-1-4335-9116-7

Library of Congress Cataloging-in-Publication Data

Names: Ferguson, Samuel D., 1982– author.
Title: Does God care about gender identity? / Samuel D. Ferguson.
Description: Wheaton, Illinois : Crossway, 2023. | Series: TGC hard questions | Includes index.
Identifiers: LCCN 2023000671 (print) | LCCN 2023000672 (ebook) | ISBN 9781433591150 (trade paperback) | ISBN 9781433591167 (pdf) | ISBN 9781433591174 (epub)
Subjects: LCSH: Church work with transgender people. | Gender identity—Religious aspects—Christianity.
Classification: LCC BV4437.6 .F47 2023 (print) | LCC BV4437.6 (ebook) | DDC 261.8/357—dc23/eng/20230419
LC record available at https://lccn.loc.gov/2023000671
LC ebook record available at https://lccn.loc.gov/2023000672

Crossway is a publishing ministry of Good News Publishers.

BP		32	31	30	29	28	27	26	25	24	23
15	14	13	12	11	10	9	8	7	6	5	4	3	2	1

Contents

"IT'S JUST BEEN SO HARD," Marie said quietly through tears. The mother of four was updating me about her eldest child's gender transition. There's no question how much Marie loves her child. Through each phase of the transition, Marie's done her utmost to remain informed, loving, and in close communication. But watching her eighteen-year-old start hormone treatments, then two years later undergo a double mastectomy, and now, at age twenty-three, struggle to manage a newly chosen identity that requires a regimen of monthly treatments, has been hard to the point of heartbreaking.

Marie and her husband first asked me to meet with them when their high school child, Skylarr,[1] announced that though biologically female, she was actually a boy. I was in the middle of doctoral work in the field of theological anthropology, studying what the Bible says about being human. My particular focus touched on areas of human embodiment and identity. I'm also a pastor with some experience walking with friends who experienced *gender dysphoria*—the technical term for severe and persistent discomfort between one's biological sex and one's psychological sense of gender.[2] Skylarr and I met at the family's house monthly for about a year. Skylarr was binding her chest and exploring masculine dress at the time. We talked a lot about what, in 2017, newscaster Katie Couric and *National Geographic* deemed the "Gender Revolution."[3]

That year, young people posed on the cover of the magazine, each one representing an emerging gender identity, including nonbinary, trans-female, androgynous, trans-male, straight female, and bigender. The cover made clear that the gender revolution was about more than a biological male being able to be a woman, or a biological female becoming a man. It marked the collapsing of a two-sexed world, the triumph of psychology over biology.

Up until the 1960s, the term *gender* was used interchangeably with *sex* to refer to the biological reality that humans are born as either male or female. These two *biological sexes* were distinguishable by their chromosomes, reproductive structures, hormone levels, and anatomical features.[4] Many modern thinkers—

including feminist psychologist Hilary Lips—still acknowledge the reality of two sexes, male and female.[5] But in recent decades, *gender* has come to mean something different from biological sex. The term as now used refers exclusively to "the psychological, social and cultural aspects of being male or female."[6] As such, peoples' *gender identity*—their self-understanding of their gender—may or may not be related to their biology. This is the revolutionary idea of the gender revolution. And with the riverbanks of biology removed, *gender identity* is now as free-flowing and expansive as one's feelings.

A recent list of gender identities includes *gender expansive* (for those who identify in a range of ways outside the male/female binary) and *gender-fluid* (for those who experience their gender identity as shifting to some extent).[7] The gender revolution is still developing, and opinions about terminology vary. But one thing is clear. The movement is sweeping, affecting areas from media to medicine, from entertainment to education, from literature to legislation. It has even affected my pastoral ministry.

A confessing Christian, Skylarr was open to exploring the biblical perspective on gender. Together we looked at the opening chapters of the Bible and talked about how, early in the biblical storyline, the reality of sexual difference, male and female, comes up. In the first chapter, we read,

> God created man in his own image,
>   in the image of God he created him;
>   male and female he created them.
>   (Gen. 1:27)

It's striking, we observed, that in a book given as part of Israel's founding, there wasn't a hint about ethnicity or nationality in the account of human beginnings. Rather, it's sexual difference that Genesis reveals as essential to humanness. Gender is at the core of who we are.

But how does the Bible understand gender? After all, the term doesn't appear in Genesis 1, nor elsewhere in Scripture. Does God's word allow for the modern divorce of biological sex and gender identity? Skylarr was convinced it does. It's possible, Skylarr thought, that a man can be born—trapped, in a sense—in a female body. "God made me a man," Skylarr told me. "But for some reason I was born in a female body, and God's call on my life is to become the man he made me to be."

Skylarr described herself as *trans**, a term that refers to someone whose gender identity doesn't align with that person's biological sex. The asterisk, as one writer explains, "is a way to refer to a variety of identities that are incredibly diverse"[8]—the spectrum of identities encompassed under the *T* in *LGBT+*. I, on the other hand, was *cisgender*, someone for whom "gender identity and birth sex are in alignment."[9] Throughout this book, I use terms like *biological sex*, *gender identity*, and *trans** with contemporary usage in mind, but I'll probe how current definitions and understandings do or do not square with biblical teaching.

After studying the Bible with Skylarr, I'd often stay for dinner. Skylarr's parents have doctoral degrees from top-tier schools and experience in the field of education. They've poured themselves into the formation of their kids. But like many parents, they felt ill-equipped to respond to their child's gender dysphoria. Worried sick for their child's well-being and longing to be supportive, they felt torn between showing a hurting adolescent compassion and offering wise leadership. The questions they asked and those that arose in my conversations with Skylarr speak for many of us left reeling by today's transgender movement.

Is it possible for a boy's mind to be trapped in a girl's body? Is there any evidence, biblically or scientifically, that gender is a purely psychological and social reality, divorced from biology? Did God design and assign our gender? Are our bodies or our minds the true guides and anchors for knowing who we are? What should we make of the novel and often irreversible practices of transitioning? What if Skylarr's feelings about her double mastectomy change in ten years?

Why This Booklet?

This booklet is written for those interested in or concerned by today's evolving views on sex and gender. It's grown out of occasions I've had as a pastor to walk with individuals who experience gender dysphoria and their families. Whether you're a Christian, a parent, or just someone curious about gender, identity, and our shared longings for transformation, I've written this book for you. I hope you'll find here compassion, clarity, and some guidance around this complex and sensitive topic.

Throughout this booklet, I will focus on two general themes: *deeper understanding* and *compassionate engagement*.

Deeper Understanding

C. S. Lewis once cautioned that a new idea "is still on trial." Before it's embraced, "it has to be tested against the great body of Christian thought down the ages, and all its hidden implications . . . have to be brought to light."[10] Certainly this holds true for the ideas that make possible the statement "It's a boy mind in a girl body."[11] For most of human history that sentence would have been unintelligible. It assumes that gender is unrelated to biology and that people can be divided into parts. These ideas have far-reaching and, when implemented, often irreversible implications.

We must be sure we understand today's transgender movement—its practices and core beliefs—and we must compare the transgender movement's ideas with how the Bible understands human beings as male or female. Similarities and differences will emerge that help us to answer three core questions: (1) Is *the body* integral or incidental to gender identity? (2) What is the *transformative path* out of dysphoria and toward wholeness? (3) Does *God* assign our biological sex and gender—that is, whether we are male or female and called to live as men or women? If so, how can we tell, and how does this affect the way we live out our maleness and femaleness?

Compassionate Engagement

In addition to seeking to understand the underlying beliefs of the transgender movement, we'll ask what biblical compassion and leadership look like when caring for someone who has come out as trans*. How should parents care for a child in duress? Can a Christian support a gender transition?

Christians should also recognize that the transgender movement provides opportunities for discipleship. What ideas about human freedom, identity, and happiness does this movement teach? Are these good for young people? Why has mental health plummeted among Generation Z as liberty for self-expression has skyrocketed? Could the rise in cases of adolescent gender dysphoria—up 1000 percent in the United States and 4000 percent in the United Kingdom[12]—owe more to social media saturation or social contagion than it does to clinical gender dysphoria? These questions relate directly to Christian growth and transformation.

Moreover, we're talking not merely about a controversial topic but about real people who are hurting and often feel misunderstood, so any engagement must be marked by compassion. As I write, I have friends in mind who have suffered greatly with gender dysphoria. I'll make a case here that many of the transgender movement's ideas and practices are unsafe, and many of its hopes ultimately false. My goal, however, is not to be callous or offensive but to set all our broken lives within the contours of Scripture's vision for humanity.

Three Core Beliefs of the Transgender Movement

The transgender revolution is sweeping. Deeper understanding of it requires us to consider three core beliefs that underly it and make it possible. Though often unarticulated, these beliefs are like the framing of a house, giving the transgender movement its present shape and stability.

Belief 1. My Identity Is Self-Determined

We can't understand the transgender movement if we don't grasp how it relates to our culture's obsession over the question *Who am I?* Traditionally, our identity was something we received, and it was therefore relatively stable. Who we are was understood as determined by family of origin, nationality, biological sex, religion, and perhaps occupation. These matters were largely "givens," arising not from feelings or decisions but from realities outside a person's control.

Things have changed. Today, identity is a do-it-yourself project based on self-discovery and self-expression.[13] This gives personal feelings and decisions pride of place, and it resists external constraint. "[Here is] a view of personhood," Carl Truman explains, "that has almost completely dispensed with the idea of any authority beyond that of personal, psychological conviction, an oddly Cartesian notion: I think I'm a woman, therefore I am a woman."[14]

Belief 2. My Feelings, Not My Body,
Determine My Gender

When I was in graduate school, a classmate named Taylor shared with me about his experience of gender dysphoria. Taylor was a biological male but, since early childhood, felt like a girl. Taylor was on a hormone treatment, experimenting with cross-dressing, and hoped to undergo transition surgery. One day Taylor asked me, "Do you feel like a man?" I answered, "Yes." Taylor fired back: "What does that mean? And don't tell me it means you like girls and sports. What does it mean to *feel* like a man?"

For years, that exchange troubled me. How do you describe the feeling of being a man—or a woman—and do so without reaching for cultural stereotypes about gender? In a culture obsessed with gender identity, I was shocked at how hard it was simply to describe what being a man feels like.

Finally, it dawned on me. Taylor's question contained a significant assumption. Taylor didn't ask me if I *was* a man. He asked me if I *felt* like a man. Subtle but seismic, this shift in verbiage reflects a core belief of the transgender movement: your feelings, not your biology, determine your identity. It's a mind-over-matter view of people, and we may be tempted to think there's nothing wrong with this way of thinking. But try applying this logic to age or race. What if a sixteen-year-old trying to buy a six-pack of beer blurts out to the vigilant clerk, "But I feel twenty-one"? What if a fifty-year-old man pursuing a sixteen-year-old girl says to her father, "But I feel sixteen"? What if a White male applying for a scholarship designated for

African Americans responds to the university examiner, "But I feel Black"?

Our society agrees—at least for now—that age and ethnic identity are determined by cold, hard facts, not feelings. You may have feelings *about* your age or ethnicity, but those feelings don't determine your age or ethnic background. Why the difference in the case of gender?

Sadly, the shift toward feeling-based identity has affected the way we care for people with mental health struggles. Skylarr told me, "My therapist is on my side." Her therapist practiced *affirmative therapy*, confirming Skylarr's psychological sense of gender and encouraging Skylarr to find ways to explore and express it.

Historically, therapists practiced *watchful waiting*, seeking to patiently understand the feelings of those who suffer from gender dysphoria while helping them become more comfortable with their biological sex. Studies indicate that most kids—roughly 70 percent—who experience childhood gender dysphoria and are not socially transitioned outgrow it.[15] Nevertheless, clinicians are under pressure to be gender affirming.[16] What does this mean for patient care? This question

leads us to the third core belief of the transgender
movement.

Belief 3. We Find Wholeness through
External, Not Internal, Change

People have long recognized their need for inner healing
and change. Humans suffer from bad thinking, broken
hearts, and any number of internal psychological disorders. But the transgender revolution's path toward healing
and wholeness assumes that the deep change a person
with gender dysphoria needs must happen mainly on the
outside. Those who suffer are told they need to change
their external appearance, not their perspective.

Increasingly, gender dysphoria is treated not through
counseling but through *transitioning*, a process that involves puberty blockers, hormone treatments, and surgeries. There's debate within the medical community as
to the age and speed at which to start a young person on
this treatment pathway. Some see a quick transition as
inappropriate and unsafe, but Dr. Colt St. Amand of the
Mayo Clinic suggests that a long assessment period before transitioning "reeks of some old kind of conversion-
therapy." The doctor goes on:

I am less concerned with certainty around identity, and more concerned with hearing the person's embodiment goals. Do you want to have a deep voice? Do you want to have breasts? You know, what do you want for your body?[17]

Even when there's debate about the timing and pace of treatment, doctors are increasingly agreed on this trajectory: *change the body to heal the mind.*

Some Concerns about Transitioning

Even if one were to grant that feelings determine gender, three major concerns arise about affirmative therapy's push for hormone and surgical transitioning.

First, affirmative therapy moves too quickly with immature kids who are easily manipulated by social pressure. Historically, gender dysphoria affected predominately males in early childhood, with a ratio as high as five boys to one girl[18]—and the majority outgrew it.[19] Today, roughly two-thirds of cases affect biological females, with symptoms arising suddenly during the turbulent years of adolescence.[20] Such changes in prevalence suggest social pressures are at play. Moreover, studies indicate that socially transitioning a child dramatically increases the likelihood gender dysphoria will persist.[21] How can we justify encouraging children during years of complex development to make permanent changes based on what may be a passing phase?

Second, the methods of transitioning are inherently traumatic to our natural bodies. One can't help but see a disconnect between our culture's growing concern for nature—care for the environment and our embrace of organic foods that aren't genetically modified—and the transgender movement's treatment of our natural bodies. One theologian put it poignantly in a letter to the [London] *Times's* editors:

> [Gender transitioning] involves denying the good-
> ness, or even the ultimate reality, of the natural
> world. Nature, however, tends to strike back, with
> the likely victims in this case being vulnerable
> and impressionable youngsters who, as confused
> adults, will pay the price for their elders' fashion-
> able fantasies.[22]

As the number of gender clinics skyrockets in the US—from one in 2007 to more than a hundred in

2022[23]—several European nations have tightened re-strictions for youth seeking to transition.[24] "The risks of hormonal interventions for gender dysphoric youth outweigh the potential benefits," said Sweden's National Board of Health and Welfare.[25]

Finally, when affirmative therapy is judged by its own stated goals, transitioning hasn't proved effective. It's not yet known whether the short-term relief from dyspho-ria teenagers can feel after transitioning will persist in adulthood.[26] Neither is it clear how teens will feel in the long run about irreversible changes made to their bodies. Grace Lidinsky-Smith's story in *Newsweek* is sobering: "One year [after transitioning], I would be curled in my bed, clutching my double-mastectomy scars and sobbing with regret."[27] Skylarr's mother shared with me post-transition, "Skylarr still knows she'll never really be a man, but she's resigned to life presenting as one." Transitioning appears to be a high-risk and often low-reward gamble.[28]

These are the core beliefs of today's transgender move-ment and some concerns they raise. Next, we'll turn to Scripture. How does the Bible understand identity and gender differently? How does it view our bodies? And for those who suffer with dysphoria, what pathways toward wholeness does Scripture offer?

Back to the Beginning

Taylor and I became friends while I studied in England. I was honored to walk alongside him as he became a Christian and sought to understand his gender dysphoria in the light of his new faith. Taylor wondered what God had to say about gender identity. Together we went back to the beginning, to the opening chapters of Genesis, and discovered these biblical truths.

Truth 1. Our Human Identity Is a Gift from Our Creator

The Bible's account of human beginnings is as much about God as it is about us. Genesis 1's emphatic message is that God is the actor in creation. Notice the verbs used throughout the creation account and who's doing the acting: "God created" (vv. 1, 21, 27), "God said" (vv. 3, 6, 9, 11, 14, 20, 24, 26), "God separated" (v. 4), "God called" (vv. 5, 8, 10), "God made" (vv. 7, 16), "God set" (v. 17), and "God blessed" (v. 28). Throughout the chapter, life is from God and according to his design.

The chapter culminates in God's creation of humanity:

> God *created* man in his own image,
>> in the image of God he *created* him;
>> male and female he *created* them.
>>> (Gen. 1:27)

The repetition of the verb "created" is striking and underscores a fundamental fact about being human: we are creatures with a Creator. A human neither determines her existence nor designs her nature. She is not her own author. Our identity—who we truly are—is God-given, not man-made. God grants people the honor of living out and cultivating their identity, but not license ultimately to design and create it.

Gloriously, Genesis 1 also reveals that the foundation of human dignity and worth lies not in biological sex, gender, ethnicity, or performance but in the fact that all people are made in God's image. This means that the process of living out our identity—though at times frustrated in a fallen world—is ultimately the unwrapping of a "very good" gift from God: "God saw *everything* that he had made, and behold, it was *very good*" (Gen. 1:31).

Truth 2. Human Beings Are Embodied,
so Gender Is Never Less Than Our Biology

Genesis 1:27 says, "Male and female he created them."
Our gender is a gift from God. But how has he given
it to us? Is gender a feeling God places *within* us, an
inner sense we discover then bring forth externally? Or
is our gender related to our bodies, grounded in our
biological sex?

The next chapter, Genesis 2, functions like a zoom
lens on the creation account. It gives us more detail
about how humankind is made as male and female.
There we see that humans are made of both physical
and spiritual realities: "The LORD God formed the man
of dust from the ground and breathed into his nostrils
the *breath of life*, and the man became a living crea-
ture" (v. 7).[29] When God made people, he knit our
physical bodies and our spirits together for eternity.[30]
Some thinkers in the ancient world imagined our
true existence as disembodied spirits. But in keeping
with the logic of creation (Gen. 1–2), the incarnation
(John 1:14), and the resurrection (Luke 24:39), the
apostle Paul insists humans are embodied and have an
embodied future (see 1 Cor. 6:19–20; 15:35–49). As

Gregg Allison puts it, "Embodiment is the proper state of human existence. God's design for his image bearers is that we are embodied people."[31]

When we speak of human identity, therefore, we must account for *all* of us. Biblically, our identity does not only come from our minds (an "inner sense") but also includes the way our bodies are made. Who we are is who and how our Creator made us. Further, when we turn to the making of the first man and woman, it's their *embodiment*, not their feelings, that determines their biological sex and gender identity.

When he forms Adam and Eve, God works with physical materials like dirt, ribs, flesh, and bone. He uses these materials to shape and build people. "God *formed* the man of dust from the ground" (Gen. 2:7). "And the rib that the LORD God had taken from the man he *made* into a woman and brought her to the man" (Gen. 2:22). The term translated "formed" here is used elsewhere to describe a potter working with clay (Isa. 45:9). The term translated "made," used to describe God shaping the woman's body, literally means "built" and is used elsewhere to describe the shaping of an altar (Ex. 17:15) and the building of a city (Num. 32:37). These passages show that the creation of humanity as male or female is inherently physical, embodied. This fact is further underscored in the description of the man and woman's "one flesh" union at the end of the chapter (Gen. 2:24), a bond that's only sensible because of the physical fit, the complementarity, of male and female bodies.

There's no sense in Genesis 1 and 2 that gender identity can be divorced from human embodiment. Therefore, there is no sense in these chapters that manhood and womanhood are merely psychological realities separable from maleness and femaleness. In a profound sense, one's body *is* one's gender. We are "gendered all the way down," Allison writes. "Every cell in a woman's body has an XX sex chromosome. Every cell in a man's body has an XY sex chromosome."[32] According to Scripture and as attested by biology, God shapes our gender into our bodies. Biological sex and gender cannot be put asunder.

Truth 3. God's Pathway for Change Is Transformation, Not Transition

The truths we discussed in Genesis 1–2 were clarifying for Taylor, but not relieving. Taylor continued to experience gender dysphoria. Learning that God writes our gender into our bodies didn't sound like good news for someone who felt such dissonance with his physical frame. Taylor's ongoing struggle meant we needed to consider the larger vista of the biblical story. Does the Bible offer a further explanation for why a person might experience gender dysphoria? Does it hold out hope for those who have such an experience?

Both the transgender movement and the Bible have a lot to say about experiences of pain. The word *dysphoria* refers to "a state of feeling very unhappy, uneasy, or dissatisfied."[33] It's the opposite of euphoria. Christians speak of "the fall," that plunge into sin, exile, and brokenness that began with Adam and Eve's rebellion in Genesis 3 and continues today. Its effects are devastating: "darkened hearts" (Rom. 1:21), "debased minds" (Rom. 1:28), "slavery to passions" (Titus 3:3), "inward groanings" (Rom. 8:23), and "wasting away" (2 Cor. 4:16). This brokenness affects all people: "All have sinned and fall short of the glory of God" (Rom. 3:23). Crime, cancer, schizophrenia, depression, barrenness, abandonment, and disease are all results of the fall.

Gender dysphoria is another painful experience of our common brokenness. As I told Taylor: "You're experiencing the fall in a particularly hard way, but the Bible is about more than brokenness and sin. It's a book about God's *triumph over* brokenness and sin."

The key term in the transgender movement, *trans**, is derived from the Latin preposition *trans*, which conveys the sense of movement "across, toward, to the farther side of, beyond."[34] It's used in the terms *transgender* and *transition*, both of which convey a desire of a person with gender dysphoria to *move from* a state of pain and incongruence *toward* one of peace and wholeness.

Our English Bibles also use the prefix *trans*, but with a different word: *transform*. Paul describes Christians this way: "We all, with unveiled face, beholding the glory of the Lord, are being *transformed* into the same image from one degree of glory to another" (2 Cor. 3:18). The Greek word we translate as "transformed" carries the meaning "to change inwardly in fundamental character or condition."[35] Christians are in a state of transformation, being *changed from* a life characterized by sin and brokenness *to* becoming more like Jesus Christ. Biblical transformation stands in stark contrast to the logic of transitioning in at least three ways.

First, transformation is from the inside out. It begins with the heart and mind, not the body. Paul writes, "Do not be conformed to this world, but be *transformed by the renewal of your mind*" (Rom. 12:2). Whereas transitioning changes the outside, transformation envisions wholeness beginning with inner change.

Second, transformation culminates when God resurrects our bodies, not when we remake them. As we see in Romans:

> We know that the whole creation has been groaning together in the pains of childbirth until now. And not only the creation, but we ourselves, who have the firstfruits of the Spirit, groan inwardly as we wait eagerly for adoption as sons, *the redemption of our bodies.* (Rom. 8:22–23)

God raises us from the dead as embodied people, and our resurrected bodies cohere with our present bodies— but in perfected form (see Phil. 3:21).[36] The resurrected Jesus appeals to his astonished disciples: "See my hands and my feet, that it is I myself. Touch me, and see. For a spirit does not have flesh and bones as you see that

I have" (Luke 24:39). Jesus was incarnate as a man and resurrected as a man. Just as the defining features of ethnicity endure into eternity (Rev. 7:9), so too does the beauty of sexual differentiation.[37]

Third, transformation is the Spirit's work in the context of Christ's new community. "The Spirit himself bears witness with our spirit that we are children of God" (Rom. 8:16). This same Spirit unifies us with other Christians: "In one Spirit we were all baptized into one body" (1 Cor. 12:13). The Spirit within us and the community around us—working through and under God's word—change us, reshaping us to be more like Christ. Christians are "born of the Spirit," "walk by the Spirit," and are "prayed for by the Spirit" (John 3:5; Rom. 8:4, 26; Gal. 5:16).

The transgender movement's agent of transition is the scalpel; Christianity's agent of transformation is the Spirit. The transgender movement sees change as primarily cosmetic, on the surface; Christians understand change to be inner and deep—it begins in the soul, moves through our character, and culminates in a perfected, imperishable, embodied existence (1 Cor. 15:42–49). A transition takes place in a clinic or on an operating table, but transformation is lived out in the context of the church, with God's people, the family of faith. The depth and thoroughness of Christian transformation mean it's no easy path. However, the Christlikeness that emerges along the way and the companionship of the Holy Spirit and fellow Christians make it a journey of ever-increasing glory and joy.

But what does transformation look like practically? How can a Christian relate to friends, family, or church members who are struggling with gender dysphoria? Given the cultural and social pressures of the transgender revolution, how can we disciple young people to think about matters of gender? With these questions in mind, we turn now from seeking deeper understanding to practicing compassionate engagement.

Encouragement for Parents

My friend Taylor once tried to explain to me what gender dysphoria felt like. "It literally hurts to be called the wrong pronouns," Taylor began, and went on to describe having trouble going out in public and the constant chafing of one's own body. I've never experienced gender dysphoria. For those like me, it's important that we respond to those who do with humility and respect. This may mean admitting we don't fully understand but committing to listening carefully and taking seriously what they're going through. This posture is particularly important with our children.

My experience walking with families touched by gender dysphoria has shown me how painful it can be for parents and siblings. When a mother suddenly learns her thirteen-year-old daughter identifies as a boy and wants to transition, hard questions follow: *Is this a passing phase or something deeper? Is it ethical, even possible, for my child to change genders? Is the science behind this trustworthy? How did this happen? What do I do?* How should parents respond when their child exclaims, "You're choosing your religion over me" or "If you don't let me transition, I'll kill myself"? Moments like these require discernment, a biblical posture and convictions, and an intentional discipleship plan. What does this look like practically? Here are eight encouragements for parents to keep in mind.

1. Show Compassion If a Child Shares a Struggle
When he encountered the sick, confused, and weary, Jesus acted with compassion (Matt 11:28–30; Mark 1:41; 6:34). So must we. Rates of depression, anxiety,

and suicide are alarmingly high among trans* youth.[38] Whatever the causes, it's clear that people who experience gender dysphoria are hurting. They may feel out of place in their own skin or experience bullying at school. Engaging a loved one or friend in such a state begins with listening, sympathy, and acknowledging that sharing about that experience took courage.[39] Christian parents should pray with a child going through this, helping the child to invite Jesus into his or her struggle.

2. Ask What Else Is Going On

For adolescents, questions about gender don't arise in a vacuum. Being a teenager has always been hard. Alongside the pressures of typical adolescent development, today's teens face the social and cultural pressures of growing up in a digital and hyper-sexualized age that obsesses over identity. For this reason, it's wise and necessary when caring for an adolescent (or adult) who identifies as trans* to consider co-occurring conditions like anxiety or depression before having any conversations about transitioning. As Mark Yarhouse and Julia Sadusky write: "We almost always recommend treating co-occurring concerns first. We do not want a person making weighty decisions about gender dysphoria out of a state of significant depression."[40] By first helping friends or loved ones address other factors that affect their mental health—anxiety or depression, difficulty with peers, or a negative body image—you may help them to grow more comfortable with their biological sex.

3. Don't Be Anxious If Your Child's Interests Aren't Stereotypical

Parents of young children shouldn't anxiously think that a son or daughter is struggling from gender dysphoria simply because the child doesn't conform to typical gender norms. After all, many modern ideals about masculinity and femininity are more cultural stereotype than biblical truth. Stereotypes can create unnecessary confusion and pressure for children as they grow up. The Bible offers contours for gender expression—especially in relation to sex and marriage—but says less than we might think about male and female preferences. Scripture doesn't say men must like sports and hunting or be unemotional. Nor does the Bible tell us that little girls must wear pink, enjoy dolls, and avoid rough-and-tumble play. If a girl likes karate, excels in math, and prefers short hair, this doesn't mean she's a boy. And if a boy likes dance, excels in art, and grows his hair out, this doesn't mean he's a girl. Sadly, gender dysphoria can, at times, be caused or increased by evaluating oneself—or being evaluated by others—according to caricatures. Kenneth Zucker notes that some of the distress associated with gender dysphoria is not inherent to the condition but reflects social rejection.[41] So, for example, if a boy feels rejected by his peers for not enjoying stereotypical boy games, he might mistake that distress for gender dysphoria.

4. Get Help If Gender Confusion Persists

Studies also show that it's not uncommon for a young child periodically to express the desire to be the opposite sex,[42] but in most cases this desire wanes with age. But what if your child's gender confusion continues into puberty and shows no signs of abating? If this is the case, your child may have a clinical case of gender dysphoria. According to the *Diagnostic and Statistical Manual of Mental Disorders* (*DSM-5*), gender dysphoria affects only a sliver of the population, less than .01 percent, or fewer than one in ten thousand people,[43] and historically affected predominately males in early childhood.[44]

In terms of clinical assessment, the American Psychiatric Association (APA) states that a child must meet six of these eight criteria for a minimum of six months to be diagnosed with gender dysphoria:

1. A strong desire to be of the other gender or an insistence that one is the other gender
2. A strong preference for wearing clothes typical of the opposite gender
3. A strong preference for cross-gender roles in make-believe play or fantasy play
4. A strong preference for the toys, games, or activities stereotypically used or engaged in by the other gender
5. A strong preference for playmates of the other gender
6. A strong rejection of toys, games, and activities typical of one's assigned gender
7. A strong dislike of one's sexual anatomy
8. A strong desire for the physical sex characteristics that match one's experienced gender[45]

Someone living with insistent, persistent, and consistent gender dysphoria will likely experience great pain. Believing parents can help their children manage by being involved in a strong Christian community, cultivating loving Christian friendships, and perhaps seeking Christian therapy or finding medical means to treat depression and anxiety.

5. Establish Clear Boundaries

To care for a child who experiences gender dysphoria, we must have clear convictions. We must guide daughters and sons toward alignment with God's creational and redemptive designs. Parents must frame their care for a child who wants to transition with the three biblical truths discussed above in view. Guidance that cuts against the grain of creation or moves away from the arc of redemption may seem palliative in the moment, but it will only increase pain in the long run. This, of course, has implications for a Christian posture toward transitioning.

An adolescent who comes out as trans* will often express urgency about beginning a transition. Some teens, like a helicopter, want to reach altitude with their transitioning straightaway. Meanwhile, cautious parents are like an airplane on the tarmac, wanting to taxi for a while.[46] But when it comes to gender, the individual is not in the pilot seat; we're all passengers. Because gender transitioning doesn't cohere with God's creational and redemptive designs, a Christian cannot affirm it. This doesn't mean we can't respect or interact with coworkers and friends who are trans*. But when it comes to our spheres of responsibility—our bodies and the bodies of our under-eighteen children—we cannot support treatments that so drastically deny God's work.

Christian parents must also be leery of soft transitioning, like cross-dressing and changing names or pronouns. Because we live in a pluralistic world, there will be situations when it's necessary, for civility's sake, to call someone by that person's preferred name.[47] But within a Christian home, parents should not support soft transitioning. A study conducted on children in the Netherlands found that soft social transitioning makes it *less* likely a child will outgrow gender dysphoria.[48] Using your child's preferred pronouns may feel low-risk, but doing so dishonors the Creator and has documented long-term effects.[49]

6. Don't Give Away Your Authority

Refusing to compromise on convictions and boundaries will put Christian parents in difficult situations. Some in our culture will judge an uncompromising response as a form of rejecting one's child.[50] There are even those who would like to see unbending parents charged with child abuse.[51] Amid such pressure, Christian parents must bear in mind their tremendous calling.

The Bible commends the wisdom and leadership of godly parents (Ex. 20:12; Prov. 1:8–9; Eph. 6:1). A child's emotions should not be their north star. God and his word must be. It's easy for parents today to think their job is to ensure their children always find happiness. But adolescence is an inherently tumultuous stage. A parent's role is setting healthy boundaries and limits. You mustn't relinquish your responsibility and authority, even if cultural pressures undermine it. Your role is to aim your child toward holiness, not painlessness—eternal joy, not immediate gratification. In this responsibility, your no is as important as your yes. Do all you can to stay in close relationship with your child, but do not neglect your biblical call to lead.

7. Guard against Negative Cultural Influences

Most cases of gender dysphoria today are not early onset diagnoses or along the lines of the *DSM-5*. Rather, they're part of a phenomenon called *rapid-onset gender dysphoria*, and many worry that the recent spike in cases is more the result of social pressure than actual struggles with gender identity. In her study of teens who came out as trans*, Lisa Littman noted two patterns among females: (1) Most adolescent girls discovered transgender ideas "out of the blue" after a period of social media saturation, and (2) "the prevalence of transgender identification within some of the girls' friend groups was more than seventy times the expected rate."[52] Littman concluded that the increase owed to "social contagion." Gender dysphoria had spread in the same way fads and rumors do, because of the social incentives gained by identifying as trans*.[53]

What should parents do if they believe their teenage child's sudden gender confusion stems more from social pressures and challenges common to adolescents than from an underlying condition? They must find the big cultural influences and intervene. Many parents have found their child's gender dysphoria dissipated when they took their child out of public school and off social media.[54]

While public education can be a great blessing, public schools increasingly discriminate against traditional and religious views of sexuality and gender. Some affirm and even aid youth in transitioning, at times without parental consent.[55] Parents must be vigilant in understanding what their children are taught in school and what policies local school systems have that may influence their children negatively. Don't hesitate to pull your children out of a school and place them into a different educational environment if you believe doing so will guard them from negative influences—whether from teachers or peers.

Social media also plays a large part in the social contagion that surrounds rapid-onset gender dysphoria.[56] This shouldn't surprise us. Social media exposes youth to the perpetual gaze and judgment of peers and other potentially negative influences. The pursuit of "likes" on platforms like Instagram can exacerbate the pressure felt by teens who may already be insecure about their changing bodies. Parents must count the cost before getting their teen a smartphone, and they shouldn't hesitate to remove access to a smartphone as a first defense against negative cultural influences when any concerns arise.[57]

8. Celebrate the Beauty and Goodness of Gendered Bodies
The beauty of gender difference adorns God's world. We need to help the next generation see and honor it. As a pastor, I have the joy of seeing couples meet, marry, and

have children. The fruit of their union reminds us that only a biological male and biological female can produce life. "People often present the sex binary as *oppressive*," writes Rebecca McLaughlin. "But at its very heart, the male-female binary is *creative*."[58] In appropriate ways, parents must teach and remind their children that the complementarity of the two-gendered world—the dance of male and female—is the creative source that stands behind each one of us. By God's design, every human being owes his or her existence to one man and one woman.[59]

Another place the beauty of gender shows up is in church worship. In my church, when songs have parts for men and women, the guys can't help but sing a little louder when it's their turn. They send a low rumble through the pews. When the women have their go, it's as if a bright and gentle joy enfolds the congregation. When all the voices finally sing together, one *hears*, even *feels*, the truth and goodness of our gendered world. Surely this will be an enduring display of our maleness and femaleness as we worship the Lamb in heaven (Rev. 5:9; 14:3; 15:3). Christians must point out this beauty to the next generation whenever we experience it. We must celebrate the goodness of God's design, that we *are* our bodies, that our gendered bodies are temples for the Holy Spirit, made to glorify God (1 Cor. 6:19–20), and that this is anything but restrictive—it's beautiful.

Encouragement for Church Leaders

1. Don't Be Silent, Teach

Marie told me that her children were learning about gender everywhere *except* from church. Topics involving the LGBT+ community are sensitive, complex, and controversial, making them difficult for pastors to address. But when churches are silent on these issues, we hand our people over to be formed by other voices. Church leaders must develop a plan to teach about God's design for sex and gender. This teaching must be applied with appropriate nuance and care in the various parts of the church where ministry takes place—from the pulpit to the classroom, from the pastor's office to a family's living room, from working with parents to teaching children.[60]

2. Foster a Culture of Support and Hope in Your Church

What if your local church were a safe place where people could be honest about their experience of gender dysphoria and find companions in suffering? Imagine these sufferers welcomed to a small group where they find support in their unique struggles. Far too many young people are pulled into the arms of the transgender movement because they find an experience of care in community there that they should've received from the church. Far too many parents live isolated in their heartbreak over a gender-confused child, needing the church to come around them in support. What if your church created support groups for both hurting individuals and hurting parents to connect, share their stories, and follow Jesus together? Choosing a life that honors our Creator and Redeemer is never easy. But the life of discipleship is good and never without God's presence (Matt. 28:20), promises (Deut. 31:8), and people (1 Cor. 12:12–13).

3. Be Aware of What's Forming Your Congregation's Youth

Pastors should be aware of what local schools are teaching about gender, at what age that teaching happens, and how they can help parents counter the unbiblical ideas children pick up there. Church leaders should also learn about which local counseling agencies support a biblical view of gender, so they can refer parents with struggling children to biblical care.

A Word for the Person Who Identifies as Trans*

Years ago, I received a call from a man we'll call Adam. He told me, "I'm in my sixties, and I recently detransitioned to life as a man after decades as a trans woman." Adam had experienced severe gender dysphoria his entire life. After years of cross-dressing at home, trying on women's clothes at T.J. Maxx, and trying but failing at several marriages, Adam finally underwent gender reassignment surgery and enjoyed several years identifying as a woman.

Adam told me that he'd heard the gospel as a teen, but he didn't immediately commit to a life of faith. "But when I got older," Adam told me, "I knew something was missing. I was missing God." Soon after that realization, Adam came across a lecture I'd given on the Bible and gender identity. "After listening to it, I went outside my house for a cigarette, and God spoke to me. It wasn't a loud voice, but a clear one in my head," Adam explained. "God said to me, 'I made you a man.'"

"With that," he told me, "it was like the fog cleared. I knew I was a man, and I knew I wanted to be with

God." Soon Adam began living a life on fire for the Lord. Adam told me he'd begun passing out gospel tracts on street corners, so I asked him, "When you were in your twenties, what could I have said to you to get you on the right path?"

"Nothing," he replied. "But what I did need was someone like you to tell me what was wrong and what was true. Keep telling people the truth." Seeds of deeper truth had been planted in Adam long ago, and even after decades of pain and confusion, they bore fruit.

If you're struggling with gender dysphoria, or if you've identified as trans*, I want you to hear the truth. The gender revolution has exposed the deeper crises of a post-Christian culture. People without God no longer know who they are. People without Christ no longer know what to do with brokenness and pain. People without the church no longer have a place to belong. But the Bible has answers for these deep questions.

Who are you? If someone had asked Paul that question, he might have replied: "I have been crucified with Christ. It is no longer I who live, but Christ who lives in me" (Gal. 2:20). Paul was *in Christ*, and it was only in this dynamic relationship with the Savior that Paul

41

was himself. In another place, he wrote, "If anyone is *in Christ*, he is a new creation" (2 Cor. 5:17). For Paul, the antidote to identity confusion is not thinking more about one's identity. Paradoxically, it's becoming increasingly consumed with the person and purposes of another, Jesus Christ. For the Christian, identity isn't so much about *who you are* but *whose you are*.

How do you deal with brokenness and pain? The antidote to gender dysphoria is not gender euphoria, finding bliss and perfection in one's gender identity. Rather, healing is found by placing one's pain at Jesus's feet and believing that in his hands, pain becomes purposeful. Paul writes: "For the sake of Christ, I am content with weaknesses, insults, hardships, persecutions, and calamities. For when I am weak, then I am strong" (2 Cor. 12:10).

Some of the most beautiful and joyful people I know are Christians who, like Paul, have suffered greatly. In their suffering, they found a doorway into intimacy with the crucified Lord. Our culture avoids pain and prizes immediate gratification, but in return, it gets purposeless sorrows and shallow joys. Even though persistent gender dysphoria may be your cross to bear in this life, following Jesus remains the only purposeful path to true life (Mark 8:34–35).

Where do you find belonging? Thankfully, pain is not our only companion in following Jesus. In Christ, Christians belong to one another (Rom. 12:5), and our loads are lighter when we shoulder them together. May a healthy local church become the supportive family you're longing for.

Does God care about your gender identity? More than you can imagine. When you were only a thought in his mind (Jer. 1:5), when he knit your body together in your mother's womb (Ps. 139:13), today, and even in your resurrected future, you have always been and always will be precious in his sight as the *man* or *woman* he designed you to be. Your body, your biological sex, is according to his design, and it reveals your gender. He wants you to root your identity in him. He wants you to identify as his son or daughter, embracing the gender he's given you and humbly aligning your heart and mind with how he's made you.

That may feel like more than you are able to accept. But the truth is that people under the spell of the gender revolution, reeling under the ache of our broken world, need more than cosmetic solutions. They need to know they belong to God. They need to know he has a purpose in their pain. They need to know they belong to his people. They need more than transition. They need transformation, a life that's shaped not by a passing movement but by the power of their almighty Creator and gracious Redeemer.

My friend Adam has gone home to be with the Lord. At his funeral, his friends shared that in the last years of his life, he continued to experience waves of gender dysphoria. But it didn't overpower him any longer. Adam knew who he was, a man made in God's image, his Father's son. Trust in Christ, and such a confidence and identity can be yours.

Notes

1. Throughout this book, I'm using pseudonyms to respect individuals' privacy. The names here reflect neither the individual's given birth name nor the later name change.

2. American Psychiatric Association, *Diagnostic and Statistical Manual of Mental Disorders*, 5th ed. (Arlington, VA: American Psychiatric Association, 2013), 451 (hereafter APA, *DSM-5*).

3. In 2017 newscasting legend Katie Couric teamed up with *National Geographic* to produce the documentary *Gender Revolution: A Journey with Katie Couric*. The film release coincided with a January 2017 *National Geographic* magazine issue also titled *Gender Revolution*.

4. There are rare instances of individuals born with atypical sexual anatomy or atypical sex chromosomes, often referred to as "intersex." For a discussion of intersex

persons, see Rebecca McLaughlin, *The Secular Creed: Engaging Five Contemporary Claims* (Austin, TX: Gospel Coalition, 2021), 95–99.

5. Hilary Lips, *Sex and Gender: An Introduction*, 6th ed. (Long Grove, IL: Waveland, 2008), 5–6, explains that *sex* refers to "a person's biological maleness or femaleness" and "is reserved for discussions of anatomy and the classification of individuals based on their anatomical category." Others, however, believe that referring to two biological sexes is limiting. As Mark A. Yarhouse and Julia A. Sadusky observe: "The latest version of the APA Publication Manual (7th ed.) recommends writers avoid terms such as *biological sex* or *natal sex* in favor of 'sex assigned at birth' or 'sex designated at birth.' . . . These terms imply [according to the manual] 'that sex is an immutable characteristic without sociocultural influence.'" Yarhouse and Sadusky, *Gender Identity and Faith: Clinical Postures, Tools, and Case Studies for Client-Centered Care*, Christian Association for Psychological Studies Books (Downers Grove, IL: IVP Academic, 2022), x.

6. See Mark Yarhouse, *Understanding Gender Dysphoria: Navigating Transgender Issues in a Changing Culture* (Downers Grove, IL: InterVarsity Press, 2015), 17. Also

see my review: Sam Ferguson, "Understanding Gender Dysphoria: Navigating Transgender Issues in a Changing Culture," TGC, July 15, 2015, https://www.thegospel coalition.org/.

7. For a detailed list of gender identities, see Mark A. Yarhouse and Julia Sadusky, *Emerging Gender Identities: Understanding the Diverse Experiences of Today's Youth* (Grand Rapids, MI: Brazos, 2020), 8–9.

8. Sam Killermann, "What Does the Asterisk in "Trans*" Stand For?," IPM, https://www.itspronouncedmetro sexual.com/2012/05/what-does-the-asterisk-in-trans -stand-for.

9. Yarhouse and Sadusky, *Emerging Gender Identities*, 8.

10. C. S. Lewis, "Introduction: On the Reading of Old Books," in Athanasius, *On the Incarnation: The Treatise "De Incarnatione Verbi Dei"* (Crestwood, NY: St. Vladimir's Seminary Press, 1996), 4.

11. This is how one girl described her two-year-old sister's insistence that she was a boy. See Petula Dvorak, "Transgender at Five," *Washington Post*, May 19, 2012.

12. The rising cases of adolescents reporting gender dysphoria is documented in several places. See Abigail Shrier, *Irreversible Damage: The Transgender Craze Seducing Our*

Daughters (Washington, DC: Regnery, 2021); M. Goodman and R. Nash, *Examining Health Outcomes for People Who Are Transgender* (Washington, DC: Patient-Centered Outcomes Research Institute, 2019), https://doi.org/10.25302/2.2019.AD.12114532; Gordon Rayner, "Minister Orders Inquiry into 4,000 Per Cent Rise in Children Wanting to Change Sex," *Telegraph*, September 16, 2018; and Emily Bazelon, "The Battle over Gender Therapy," *New York Times*, June 24, 2022.

13. Brian Rosner, *How to Find Yourself: Why Looking Inward Is Not the Answer* (Wheaton, IL: Crossway, 2022), 16.

14. Carl Trueman, *The Rise and Triumph of the Modern Self: Cultural Amnesia, Expressive Individualism, and the Road to Sexual Revolution* (Wheaton, IL: Crossway, 2020), 36.

15. Shrier, *Irreversible Damage*, 119.

16. The American Academy of Pediatrics describes watchful waiting as "outdated" (Yarhouse and Sadusky, *Gender Identity and Faith*, 54), and the American Psychological Association encourages psychologists to "adapt or modify their understanding of gender, broadening the range of variation viewed as healthy and normative" (Shrier, *Irreversible Damage*, 99).

17. Bazelon, "The Battle over Gender Therapy."

18. Yarhouse and Sadusky, *Gender Identity and Faith*, 78.

19. Shrier, *Irreversible Damage*, 119, notes, "Several studies indicate that nearly 70 percent of kids who experience childhood gender dysphoria—and are not affirmed or socially transitioned—eventually outgrow it."

20. Shrier, *Irreversible Damage*, 26, and Bazelon, "The Battle over Gender Therapy." Bazelon notes that "two-thirds" of the current caseload involves biological females.

21. Kenneth J. Zucker, "Debate: Different Strokes for Different Folks," *Child and Adolescent Mental Health* 25, no. 1 (2020): 36–37.

22. N. T. Wright, letter to the editor, *Times* (UK), August 3, 2017, https://www.thetimes.co.uk/.

23. Chad Terhune, Robin Respaut, and Michelle Conlin, "As More Transgender Children Seek Medical Care, Families Confront Many Unknowns," Reuters, October 6, 2022, https://www.reuters.com/investigates/.

24. Bazelon, "The Battle over Gender Therapy," writes, "As the United States battled over whether gender-related care should be banned or made more accessible, a few European countries that had some liberal practices concerning young people seeking medication imposed new limits recently."

25. "Summary of Key Recommendations from the Swed-ish National Board of Health and Welfare," SEGM, February 27, 2022, https://segm.org/segm-summary-sweden-prioritizes-therapy-curbs-hormones-for-gender-dysphoric-youth.

26. Bazelon, "The Battle over Gender Therapy."

27. Grace Lidinsky-Smith, "There's No Standard for Care When It Comes to Trans Medicine," *Newsweek*, June 25, 2021, https://www.newsweek.com/.

28. In the UK, one gender clinic hid reports that showed rates of self-harm and suicide did not decrease after adolescent girls were put on puberty blockers. Shrier, *Irreversible Damage*, 118.

29. That fact that "breath of life" refers to a spiritual dynamic in humans is made clear in the book of Job: "But it is the spirit in man, / the breath of the Almighty, that makes him understand" (Job 32:8; see also Job 33:4).

30. As John Paul II wrote: "Man is a person in the unity of his body and his spirit. The body can never be reduced to mere matter: It is a spiritualized body, just as man's spirit is so closely united to the body that he can be described as an embodied spirit." John Paul II, *Man and Woman He Created Them: A Theology of the Body* (Boston, MA: Pauline Books &

Media, 2006), 96. See also Edmund Fong, "Could God Misplace a Female Soul in a Male Body? Gender Identity and Contemporary Models of Human Constitution," TGC, August 25, 2022, https://www.thegospelcoalition.org/.

31. Gregg R. Allison, *Embodied: Living as Whole People in a Fractured World* (Grand Rapids, MI: Baker, 2021), 17. See also N. T. Wright, "Mind, Spirit, Soul and Body: All for One and One for All Reflections on Paul's Anthropology in His Complex Contexts," https://ntwrightpage.com/2016/07/12/mind-spirit-soul-and-body/.

32. Allison, *Embodied*, 45.

33. "Dysphoria," *Merriam-Webster Dictionary*, https://www.merriam-webster.com/dictionary/dysphoria.

34. "Trans," *The Compact Oxford English Dictionary*, 2nd ed. (Oxford: Clarendon, 1998), 2095.

35. "μεταμορφόω," Frederick W. Danker, Walter Bauer, William F. Arndt, and F. Wilbur Gingrich, *Greek-English Lexicon of the New Testament and Other Early Christian Literature*, 3rd ed. (Chicago: University of Chicago Press, 2000), 639.

36. Sam Allberry, *What God Has to Say about Our Bodies: How the Gospel Is Good News for Our Physical Selves* (Wheaton, IL: Crossway, 2021), 182.

37. Some, citing Jesus's teaching that we won't marry in heaven (Matt. 22:30), have wondered whether we will be male and female in the eschaton. But when we consider Jesus's bodily appearances and that ethnicity endures into the new heavens and new earth, it seems reasonable to believe gendered bodies remain as well.

38. J. L. Turban, A. L. C. de Vries, K. J. Zucker, and S. Shadianloo, "Transgender and Gender Non-conforming Youth," in *IACAPAP e-Textbook of Child and Adolescent Mental Health*, ed. J. M. Rey (Geneva: International Association for Child and Adolescent Psychiatry and Allied Professions, 2018), https://www.academia.edu/48889569/. See also C. Dhejne, R. Van Vlerken, G. Heylens, and J. Arcelus, "Mental Health and Gender Dysphoria: A Review of the Literature," *International Review of Psychiatry* 28, no. 1 (2016): 44–57, and Shrier, *Irreversible Damage*, 117.

39. Jared Kennedy, *A Parent's Guide to Teaching Your Children about Gender: Helping Kids Navigate a Confusing Culture* (Washington, DC: Leland House, 2020), 40–42.

40. Yarhouse and Sadusky, *Gender Identity and Faith*, 47.

41. See Kenneth Zucker, "Gender Identity Disorder in Children and Adolescents," 467–92, cited by Yarhouse, *Understanding Gender Dysphoria*, 93.

42. K. J. Zucker, S. J. Bradley, and M. Sanikhani, "Sex Difference in Referral Rates of Children with Gender Identity Disorder: Some Hypotheses," *Journal of Abnormal Child Psychology* 25, no. 3 (1997): 217–27.

43. APA, *DSM-5*, 454, "For natal adult males, prevalence [of gender dysphoria] ranges from 0.005% to 0.014%, and for natal females, from 0.002% to 0.003%."

44. Yarhouse and Sadusky, *Gender Identity and Faith*, 78; see also footnote 17.

45. APA, *DSM-5*, 452.

46. Cf. Yarhouse and Sadusky, *Gender Identity and Faith*, 80.

47. As Andrew Walker suggests, it's preferable when possible to call gender nonconforming individuals by their preferred name "because names are not as objectively gendered." Andrew T. Walker, *God and the Transgender Debate: What Does the Bible Actually Say about Gender Identity?*, 2nd ed. (Charlotte, NC: Good Book, 2022), 157.

48. T. D. Steensma, R. Biemond, F. de Boer, and P. T. Cohen-Kettenis, "Desisting and Persisting Gender Dysphoria after Childhood: A Qualitative Follow-up Study," *Clinical Child Psychology and Psychiatry* 16, no. 4 (2011): 499–516. "[A] number of girls," the researchers write, "indicated that going back to their actual gender

role was a troublesome and arduous process," even when they wanted to desist. Cited in Shrier, *Irreversible Damage*, 115.

49. Zucker, "Debate," 36–37.

50. Bazelon, "The Battle over Gender Therapy," writes about how the Family Acceptance Project, a research and intervention program for families of LGBT children, tells parents that "refusing to use a child's chosen names and pronouns is a form of rejection."

51. Laura Vozzella and Gregory Schneider, "LGBTQ Bill on Child Abuse Creates Uproar in Virginia and Beyond," *Washington Post*, October 14, 2022.

52. Lisa Littman, "Parent Reports of Adolescents and Young Adults Perceived to Show Signs of a Rapid Onset of Gender Dysphoria," PLOS ONE 13, no. 8 (2018), https://doi.org/10.1371/journal.pone.0202330. Her work is helpfully summarized in Shrier, *Irreversible Damage*, 26.

53. Littman, "Parent Reports."

54. For one family's story, see Sarah Eekhoff Zylstra, "Transformation of a Transgender Youth," TGC, July 6, 2022, https://www.thegospelcoalition.org/.

55. Schrier, *Irreversible Damage*, 59. Also see Tony Perkins, "The Secret Life of Wisconsin Kids," Family Research

Council, February 20, 2020, https://www.frc.org/; Peter Hasson, "Michigan Schools to Let Students Choose Gender, Name and Bathroom," Daily Caller, March 21, 2016, https://dailycaller.com/; Adam Clark, "New Jersey Schools Can Keep Transgender Kids' Secret from Parents, State Says," NJ.com, October 7, 2018, https://www.nj.com/; and Perkins, "Calif. Schools: Hormones through Homeroom?," Family Research Council, February, 21, 2020, https://www.frc.org/.

56. See Littman, "Parent Reports."

57. Shrier, *Irreversible Damage*, 212.

58. McLaughlin, *The Secular Creed*, 96, emphasis original.

59. Two insightful articles on the beauty of sexual difference as displayed in Scripture are Andrew Wilson, "Beautiful Difference: The (Whole-Bible) Complementarity of Male and Female," TGC, May 20, 2021, https://www.thegospelcoalition.org/, and Patrick Schreiner, "Man and Woman: Toward an Ontology," *eikon: A Journal for Biblical Anthropology* 2, no. 2 (2020), https://cbmw.org/2020/11/20/man-and-woman-toward-an-ontology.

60. Though imperfectly, my church has done this through a sermon miniseries, "Mere Sexuality"; a weekend conference,

"Being Human: Gender, Sexuality, Fulfillment"; and some evening seminars for parents that involve teaching and much time for questions and answers. Find the seminar at the Falls Church Anglican website, https://www.tfcanglican.org/being-human; find the sermon series at https://www.tfcanglican.org/sermons-1/2021/mere-sexuality.

Glossary

androgynous. Expressing gender in ways that omit markers of masculinity and femininity or mix them.

affirmative therapy. A method of treatment that confirms an individual's psychological sense of gender and encourages ways to explore and express it.

biological (or natal) sex. The sum of binary differences between male and female distinguishable by chromosomes, reproductive structures, hormone levels, and anatomical features.

cisgender. Of or relating to someone for whom gender identity and biological sex are in alignment.

gender. Up until the 1960s, used interchangeably with the term *sex* to refer to the biological reality that humans are born as either male or female. Now used exclusively to refer to the psychological, social, and cultural aspects of being male or female.

gender dysphoria. Severe and persistent discomfort between one's biological sex and one's psychological sense of gender.

gender expansive. Identifying in a range of ways outside the male/female binary.

gender expression. The way a person expresses gender identity through behavior, dress, speech, activities, mannerism, and more.

gender-fluid. Experiencing one's gender identity as shifting to some extent.

gender identity. A person's self-understanding regarding gender.

gender transition. A process by which transgender persons comes to live in accordance with their psychological sense of gender through changes to their appearance and presentation. Often this involves the aid of medical procedures and therapies that include puberty blockers, hormone treatments, and surgeries.

nonbinary. Of or relating to people whose gender identity doesn't sit comfortably with either "man" or "woman." Nonbinary identities vary and can include particular aspects of binary identities or reject them entirely.

soft transition. A process of adopting aspects of a gender transition, like cross-dressing or changing names and pronouns, that do not involve medical procedures.

trans*. Of or relating to someone whose gender identity differs from that person's biological sex. The asterisk refers to the diverse spectrum of identities encompassed under the *T* in *LGBT+*.

trans man. A person identifying as a man whose biological sex is female.

trans woman. A person identifying as a woman whose biological sex is male.

transgender. Of or relating to someone whose gender identity differs from that person's biological sex. Unlike the term *trans**, this term is typically used for people whose gender identity aligns with the opposite sex (e.g., trans-female or trans-male).

watchful waiting. Seeking to patiently understand the feelings of those who suffer from gender dysphoria while helping them become more comfortable with their biological sex.

Recommended Resources

Allberry, Sam. *What God Has to Say about Our Bodies: How the Gospel Is Good News for Our Physical Selves*. Wheaton, IL: Crossway, 2021. Both the sexual and the gender revolutions have exposed the church's lack of clear teaching about human embodiment. This book offers a deep and accessible account of biblical teaching about our bodies, showing that we are our bodies and that what we do with them matters.

Allison, Gregg R. *Embodied: Living as Whole People in a Fractured World*. Grand Rapids, MI: Baker, 2021. Written by a world-class biblical scholar, this book helps Christians think about how the truth that God made our bodies informs our views of gender, brokenness, death, and even our future, resurrected life.

Ryan T. Anderson, *When Harry Became Sally: Responding to the Transgender Moment* (New York: Encounter, 2019).

Written by a brilliant thinker and public intellectual, this deeply researched work exposes pitfalls of the transgender movement from an array of angles: cultural, philosophical, biological, policy related, and more. There is also a pastoral element, as Anderson engages compassionately with stories of those who've detransitioned and offers a hopeful vision of the goodness of God-given maleness and femaleness.

Bunt, Andrew. *Finding Your Best Identity: A Short Christian Introduction to Identity, Sexuality, and Gender.* Downers Grove, IL: InterVarsity Press, 2022. Written from the perspective of someone who has struggled with his gender identity, this book guides readers along a biblical path toward understanding and developing a God-given identity.

Kennedy, Jared. *A Parent's Guide to Teaching Your Children about Gender: Helping Kids Navigate a Confusing Culture.* Washington, DC: Leland House, 2020. Biblical and practical, this is a helpful tool for parents as they consider the how, when, and what of teaching their children about gender.

Roberts, Vaughan. *Transgender.* Talking Points. Charlotte, NC: Good Book, 2016. A short and accessible account of the gender revolution and why its views don't square with Scripture.

Shrier, Abigail. *Irreversible Damage: The Transgender Craze Seducing Our Daughters*. Washington, DC: Regnery, 2021. This book offers a non-Christian account of the negative and dangerous effects of the gender revolution. Filled with interviews and firsthand accounts, it's a powerful testimony of the dangers today's gender movement poses to children and teens.

Walker, Andrew T. *God and the Transgender Debate: What Does the Bible Actually Say about Gender Identity?* 2nd ed. Charlotte, NC: Good Book, 2022. A thorough and biblical overview of the beliefs of the gender movement, how Scripture differs, and how Christians can respond thoughtfully and faithfully.

Scripture Index

TGC | THE GOSPEL COALITION

The Gospel Coalition (TGC) supports the church in making disciples of all nations, by providing gospel-centered resources that are trusted and timely, winsome and wise.

Guided by a Council of more than 40 pastors in the Reformed tradition, TGC seeks to advance gospel-centered ministry for the next generation by producing content (including articles, podcasts, videos, courses, and books) and convening leaders (including conferences, virtual events, training, and regional chapters).

In all of this we want to help Christians around the world better grasp the gospel of Jesus Christ and apply it to all of life in the 21st century. We want to offer biblical truth in an era of great confusion. We want to offer gospel-centered hope for the searching.

Join us by visiting TGC.org so you can be equipped to love God with all your heart, soul, mind, and strength, and to love your neighbor as yourself.

TGC.org

TGC Hard Questions Series

Does God Care about Gender Identity?

Samuel D. Ferguson

Is Christianity Good for the World?

Sharon James

Why Do We Feel Lonely at Church?

Jeremy Linneman

TGC Hard Questions is a series of short
booklets that seek to answer common
but difficult questions people ask about
Christianity. The series serves the church
by providing tools that answer unchurched
people's deep longings for community, their
concerns about biblical ethics, and their
doubts about confessional faith.

For more information, visit **crossway.org**.

Also Available from the Gospel Coalition

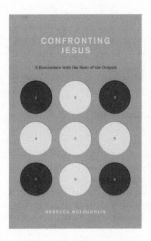

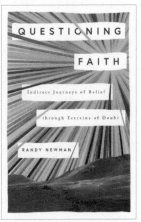

For more information, visit **crossway.org**.